DK DORLING KINDERSLEY *READERS*

Level 1

A Day at Greenhill Farm
Truck Trouble
Tale of a Tadpole
Surprise Puppy!
Duckling Days
A Day at Seagull Beach
Whatever the Weather
Busy Buzzy Bee
Big Machines
Wild Baby Animals
LEGO: Trouble at the Bridge
A Bed for the Winter
Born to be a Butterfly
A Dinosaur's Day

Level 2

Dinosaur Dinners
Fire Fighter!
Bugs! Bugs! Bugs!
Slinky, Scaly Snakes!
Animal Hospital
The Little Ballerina
Munching, Crunching, Sniffing
    and Snooping
The Secret Life of Trees
Winking, Blinking, Wiggling
    and Waggling
Astronaut – Living in Space
LEGO: Castle Under Attack!
Twisters!
Holiday! Celebration Days
    around the World
The Story of Pocahontas

Level 3

Spacebusters
Beastly Tales
Shark Attack!
Titanic

Invaders from Outer Space
Movie Magic
Plants Bite Back!
Time Traveler
Bermuda Triangle
Tiger Tales
Aladdin
Heidi
LEGO: Mission to the Arctic
Zeppelin – The Age of
    the Airship
Spies
Terror on the Amazon
NFL: Troy Aikman
NFL: Super Bowl Heroes

Level 4

Days of the Knights
Volcanoes
Secrets of the Mummies
Pirates!
Horse Heroes
Trojan Horse
Micromonsters
Going for Gold!
Extreme Machines
Flying Ace – The Story of
    Amelia Earhart
Robin Hood
Black Beauty
LEGO: Race for Survival
Free at Last! The Story of
    Martin Luther King, Jr.
Joan of Arc
Spooky Spinechillers
Welcome to The Globe! The Story
    of Shakespeare's Theater
NFL: NFL's Greatest Upsets
NFL: Terrell Davis

DORLING KINDERSLEY READERS

PROFICIENT
4
READERS

TERRELL
DAVIS
SUPERSTAR
RUNNING BACK

Written by Brian C. Peterson

A Dorling Kindersley Book

Meet T.D.

The Denver Broncos' Terrell Davis is one of the best and most exciting players in the National Football League (NFL).

The 5-foot 11-inch, 211-pound running back is both strong and quick. He also excels at finding open holes, then running over opposing defenders.

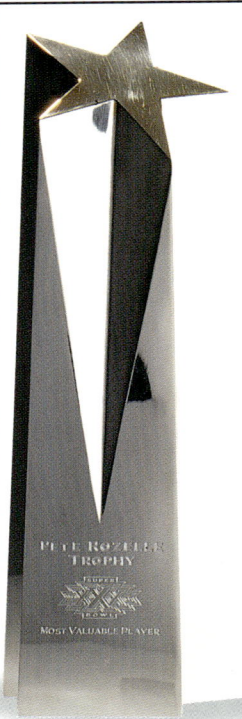

MVP!
Terrell Davis won the Pete Rozelle Trophy as the most valuable player of Super Bowl XXXII.

Leader
Terrell led the American Football Conference (AFC) in rushing three times.

Terrell was named the NFL's most valuable player in 1998, earned the MVP award in Super Bowl XXXII, and is one of four players in NFL history to run for more than 2,000 yards in one season.

A three-time Pro Bowl selection, he has rushed for 6,624 yards and averaged more than 100 yards per game during his NFL career. He has also helped the Broncos make the playoffs three times in five years.

His career highlights are victories in Super Bowls XXXII and XXXIII.

However, Terrell wasn't always a superstar. He wasn't a great athlete when he was young, and he grew up poor in a rough neighborhood. He overcame a lot of obstacles to make it in the NFL.

This is his story.

Super ball
Super Bowl games use specially stamped balls, like this one from Denver's Super Bowl XXXII victory.

Super Bowl numbers
Super Bowl games are identified using Roman numerals. For instance, X equals 10, V equals 5, and I equals 1. So Super Bowl XXXIII is the 33rd game.

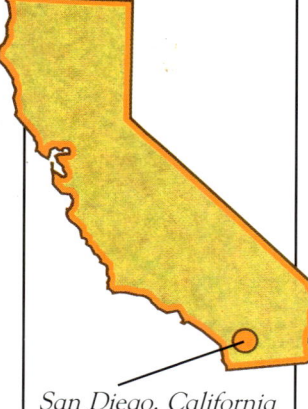

San Diego, California

Sweet home San Diego

In 1972, John and Kateree Davis and their five boys moved from St. Louis, Missouri, to San Diego, California.

Kateree decided to move to San Diego after her grandfather Nishel Thomas wrote her letters about the sunshine and palm trees in southern California. Nishel had helped raise Kateree when she was growing up.

Two months after Kateree arrived in San Diego, she gave birth to her sixth boy, Terrell [tuh-RELL].

Terrell was born on October 28, 1972. He was named after a noted rhythm and blues singer, Tammi Terrell, who had a hit duet with Marvin Gaye called "Ain't Nothin' Like the Real Thing."

Life was not easy for the Davis family when Terrell was young. His father, John, who was nicknamed "Joe," had a troubled past.

Joe had spent time in prison and was an alcoholic. But although he had had a tough life, Joe still did his best to support his family. He worked as a welder, and he cared for his kids and taught them to be tough and disciplined.

Namesake
Terrell Davis was named for the singer Tammi Terrell, who performed in the 1960s.

Star shot
This photograph of Terrell and his mother ran in *Sports Illustrated* magazine.

Brothers
The Davis brothers (left to right): Terrell, Joe, Jr., Reggie, Terry, and Bobby. Missing from the photo is James.

In San Diego, Kateree went to school and found work as an assistant at a nursing home. She was a kind-hearted person who gave everything she had to her children.

"My mom is my hero," Terrell said. "She is the most important person in my life. And the most loving and giving person I know."

The Davis family owned a five-bedroom house on Latimer Street.

The house was in southeast San Diego in a poor neighborhood. Even though the Davis family didn't have a lot of money, there was enough to eat.

Most important, they knew how to have fun together. Terrell and his family liked to listen to Motown musicians such as Al Green, the Temptations, and the Four Tops.

Hero I
James Brooks played for San Diego from 1981 to 1983 and then for the Cincinnati Bengals.

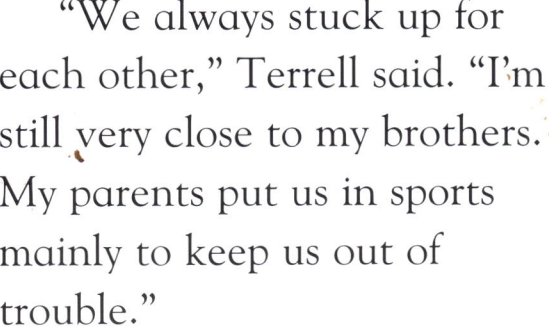

"We always stuck up for each other," Terrell said. "I'm still very close to my brothers. My parents put us in sports mainly to keep us out of trouble."

As a kid, Terrell had pictures of San Diego Chargers football players on the walls of his room. His favorite players were Chargers running backs James Brooks and Chuck Muncie.

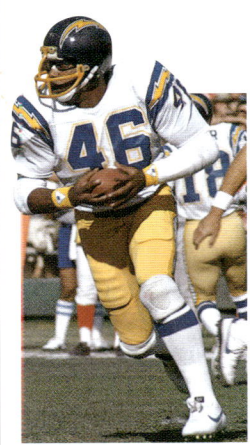

Hero II
After playing with the New Orleans Saints, Chuck Muncie was with San Diego from 1980 to 1984.

When Terrell was seven years old he played in a Pop Warner football league at Martin Luther King Park near his home. Terrell was a very good running back.

His Pop Warner coach, Frank White, owned a Cadillac. Frank said Terrell looked like the

character "Boss Hogg" from the *Dukes of Hazzard* television show when Terrell would ride in the back seat of the Cadillac. So Frank nicknamed Terrell "Boss Hogg."

When Terrell was 14 years old, his father died of a muscle disease called lupus [LOO-pus]. Terrell's father was only 41 years old. Terrell was very sad and soon became withdrawn.

"I still remember looking at Pops the day he died," Terrell said. "I'd never seen a dead person before. I wanted Pops to get up! Say something! I thought, 'This can't be happening.'"

Terrell quit football after his dad died. He didn't get good grades in school. And he quit his job delivering newspapers on the paper route he had had since he was five years old.

Paper route
Many newspapers employ young people to deliver papers to homes and businesses. The area they deliver to is called their route.

Kid star
Terrell played several positions in Pop Warner football.

Terrell attended Morse High School in San Diego for two years before he transferred to Lincoln High School in 1988.

"I'd never felt more lost in my life than when I was at Morse," Terrell said several years later.

Heisman Trophy
The Heisman Trophy goes to the nation's top college football player.

Stinger
Hornets are insects related to wasps. They live in nests and have sharp stingers.

Terrell (7) was a solid player in high school but not a star.

At Lincoln, Terrell changed his outlook on life. He was going to school with a lot of his old friends, especially Jamaul Pennington, who had lived with Terrell's family for a while.

Jamaul encouraged Terrell to go out for football at Lincoln.

Lincoln's football team was named the Hornets, and had been successful. Former NFL superstar running back Marcus Allen had played for Lincoln, leading the Hornets to the San Diego city championship.

In 1981, Allen went on to win the Heisman Trophy at the University of Southern California (USC) and was named the MVP of Super Bowl XVIII with the Raiders.

Allen retired in 1997 with 123 career rushing touchdowns, second most all-time in the NFL.

Marcus Allen
Allen starred at running back for the Raiders and Chiefs from 1982 to 1997.

MARCUS ALLEN
1981
HEISMAN TROPHY WINNER

Just in case
After joining the NFL, Terrell returned to Lincoln High for a visit and posed in front of Marcus Allen's trophy case.

"I remember looking at the trophy case that had Marcus's high school jersey in it and saying, 'Wow! I can't believe he did all that stuff,'" Terrell said. "Never did I think that I could be that successful."

Terrell was not a star football player in high school. He weighed 190 pounds and played nose guard on the defensive line, guard on the offensive line, and fullback.

Most offensive and defensive linemen in college and in the NFL now weigh nearly 300 pounds.

Terrell was better in track and field. He set school records in the discus throw and 440-yard run.

His favorite memory of playing high school football was when the team went on a week-long trip to Washington, D.C. Terrell had never been that far away from home.

"I didn't think football was going to take me anywhere," Terrell said. "A 190-pound fullback and nose guard? Where is that going to take you? Nowhere!

"My aunt was an accountant, and I thought what she did was exciting," Terrell said. "I liked math and working with numbers. I thought accounting or finance would make a good career."

But accounting would have to wait. Terrell was off to college.

Discus
Based on an ancient Greek design, the discus is thrown for distance at track and field meets. It weighs about 4½ pounds.

Accounting
This profession works with finances and money, ensuring accurate record-keeping by families and businesses.

At the beach
Terrell played football at Long Beach State, which is located south of Los Angeles, California.

Pro coach
Before coaching Terrell in college, George Allen coached the Redskins (above) and Rams in the NFL.

T.D. goes to college

Terrell Davis's older brother, Reggie, was the person most responsible for getting Terrell a football scholarship to Long Beach State University in Southern California.

Reggie convinced Long Beach State head coach George Allen (right) to take a chance on Terrell.

Allen had been a successful NFL head coach for 12 years before taking over at Long Beach State. It didn't take Allen long to see that Terrell was a special player.

"My entire outlook on my future changed under Coach Allen," Terrell said. "When I first got to Long Beach, I played on the scout team and performed really well against the first team. Coach Allen started giving me nicknames. He called me 'Secretariat' after the legendary race horse.

"After my first year, there were stories in the paper in which coach Allen said that I was a player to watch. He had coached in the pros, and he knew I could make it in the NFL."

Allen died in 1990, and Long Beach State dropped its football program in 1991. With no team to play for, Terrell had to transfer, which means move to another college. He decided to transfer across the country to the University of Georgia.

Coach Allen had a big influence on Terrell at Long Beach State.

Bulldog
Georgia athletic teams are named for this tough-looking dog.

The Georgia Bulldogs gave Terrell a chance to prove he could play on a higher level.

However, from 1992 to 1995, Terrell played in the shadow of running back Garrison Hearst and quarterback Eric Zeier. He also missed several games due to minor injuries.

Hearst got the attention of NFL scouts and went on to become a first-round selection of the Arizona Cardinals in 1993.

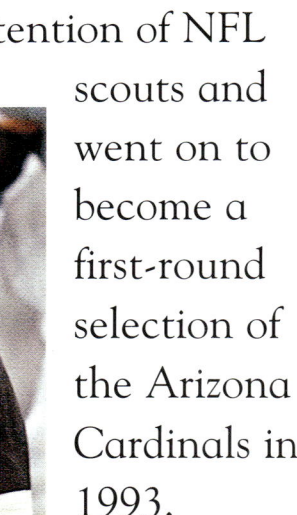

Terrell ran for more than 1,600 yards in three seasons at Georgia.

Zeier was a second-round choice of the Cleveland Browns in 1995.

Terrell was used to other players getting most of the attention, however, so it didn't bother him.

But a truly terrible moment in Terrell's college career came when he learned his close friend Jamaul Pennington had been shot and killed in San Diego.

"I began thinking anything's possible in this world," Terrell said. "Anything. Bad or good. Anything."

Terrell learned that anything was indeed possible when the Denver Broncos made him their sixth-round pick in the 1995 NFL draft. That he was chosen by an NFL team at all was a big surprise.

The Broncos' scouts thought Terrell had talent, but most NFL teams didn't know much about Terrell. He was a solid player, but those missed games hurt his case.

Georgia stars Garrison Hearst (top) is now a running back with the San Francisco 49ers. Eric Zeier (below) played for Tampa Bay.

NFL Draft
NFL teams select college players to join their teams in this annual event, held each April in New York City.

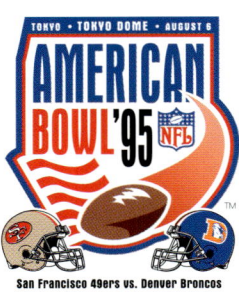

San Francisco 49ers vs. Denver Broncos

NFL goes international
Since 1989, NFL teams have played preseason games in other countries. The games are called American Bowls.

Although his NFL dream had come true, Terrell was not thrilled. That was because late-round draft picks usually have a very difficult time making an NFL team. Terrell had hoped to go undrafted and become a free agent. That way he could pick where he wanted to play.

"I'm not going to lie," Terrell said. "I was upset about Denver.

"At the start of training camp, I wasn't getting much of a chance to play, and I thought I'd be going home to San Diego pretty soon."

Tokyo Dome
This enormous stadium in Tokyo, Japan, seats more than 50,000 spectators.

As a rookie, Terrell got his first chance to show people just how good he was in a preseason game against the San Francisco 49ers. The game was played in Tokyo, Japan.

Terrell saw his first game action on special teams. His job on the kickoff team was to run as fast as he could down the field and tackle the opposing kick returner.

Special teams
These units of a football team are on the field during kicks, punts, and field-goal and extra-point attempts.

Terrell did such a good job in the game against the 49ers that he was voted the Broncos' special-teams player of the week.

Tight end
Terrell's teammate Shannon Sharpe was the top tight end (a position that combines blocking and receiving) in the NFL in the 1990s.

Rookie
A player in his first year with a pro sports team is called a rookie.

"Terrell went down on that kickoff and just blew up the return guy," former Broncos tight end Shannon Sharpe said. "Terrell knocked him back fifteen feet. We looked at each other on the sideline and said, 'We have a player here.'"

Terrell also got his first opportunity to play running back against the 49ers. He ran the ball 11 times for 47 yards.

Terrell went on to lead the team in rushing during the preseason and won the starting job for the Broncos in September.

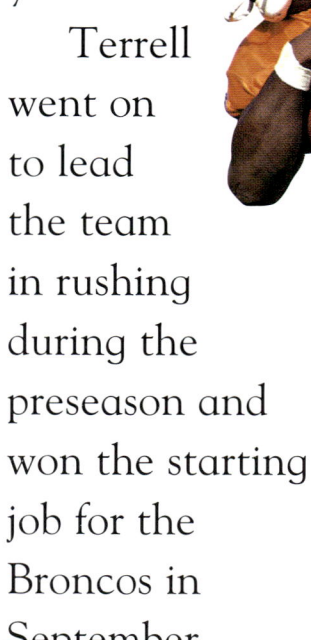

He gained 1,117 rushing yards in 1995 and became the lowest-drafted player in NFL history to rush for more than 1,000 yards as a rookie.

Football Digest magazine selected Terrell as the 1995 rookie of the year.

"Terrell's past is what drives him,"

In orange Terrell's first uniform with Denver was this orange jersey. In 1997, the team switched to dark blue jerseys.

Broncos wide receiver Rod Smith said. "No matter how much success he has, the guy still feels the need to prove people wrong because he seemed to come out of nowhere to succeed in the NFL.

"He had to be tough. All he ever heard when he was coming up was that he couldn't make it."

Terrell continued to work hard to prove them wrong.

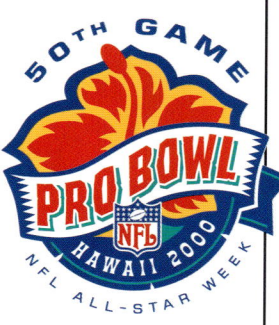

Pro Bowl
The NFL's annual postseason all-star game is held each February in Honolulu, Hawaii. Terrell has played in three Pro Bowls (1997, below).

The first Super season

In 1996, the Denver Broncos finished the regular season 13-3, which tied for the best record in the NFL. They earned a spot in the NFL playoffs.

Terrell Davis was even better in 1996 than he was in 1995. He set club records for rushing yards (1,538), total yards from scrimmage (1,848), and touchdowns (15) in a season.

Sports Illustrated magazine named him the NFL's most valuable player, and he was chosen to play in his first Pro Bowl.

However, the Jacksonville Jaguars upset the Broncos 30-27 in Denver in the first round of the playoffs.

The Broncos and Terrell were determined not to let that happen again in 1997. They knew that they could get to the Super Bowl.

Terrell and his teammates showed how serious they were about playing in the Super Bowl by inventing the Mile High Salute during training camp in 1997.

The Mile High Salute was a way for the running backs to thank each other for hard work and to celebrate making big plays.

Salute! Terrell and teammate Howard Griffith demonstrate the Broncos' Mile High Salute after Davis scored a touchdown in Super Bowl XXXII.

John Elway
Denver's superstar quarterback led the team from 1983 to 1997, helping them to five Super Bowls.

Wild card
A team that doesn't win its division but has a good enough record to make the playoffs is called a "wild-card" team.

Whenever Terrell made a big play or scored a touchdown, he jumped up and gave a military-style salute to his nearest teammates.

"Like in war, football players are asked to do some crazy stuff," Terrell said. "Football is combat without weapons. We believed we were like soldiers and there was no limit to what we could accomplish."

All the players on the team began giving the Mile High Salute when the Broncos opened the 1997 season with a six-game winning streak.

Broncos quarterback John Elway was the main weapon in the passing attack. Terrell was the driving force in the running game.

He ran for more than 200 yards in a game twice, with 215 yards against the Cincinnati Bengals (right) and 207 against the Buffalo Bills.

Terrell led the AFC with 1,750 rushing yards, setting a Broncos' single-season record.

The Broncos and Terrell seemed unstoppable. But Denver lost two of its final three games and finished in second place in the AFC West.

Despite being a wild-card playoff team, the Broncos soon proved they were the best team in the NFL.

Denver's home
The Broncos' home is called Mile High Stadium because the elevation of Denver is one mile above sea level.

They got revenge on the Jaguars by defeating them 42-17 in a wild-card playoff game.

Terrell played brilliantly. He ran for 184 yards and two touchdowns in just the first three quarters. Terrell bruised his ribs in the third quarter and left the game.

Jumping the Jaguars
Before leaving with an injury, Terrell set a Denver playoff record with 184 rushing yards.

In the AFC divisional playoffs, Terrell scored two touchdowns in the Broncos' 14-10 victory at Kansas City. Terrell also rushed for 101 yards on a very cold day.

Denver traveled to Pittsburgh for the AFC Championship Game, where Terrell again showed his greatness. He rushed for 139 yards and a touchdown as the Broncos won 24-21.

They advanced to Super Bowl XXXII against the defending Super Bowl-champion Green Bay Packers.

"We have a team that likes to run the ball," Terrell said. "It's what we do. We don't look at who's on the other side of the ball. We don't change our game plan for the opponent."

Right from the start of Super Bowl XXXII, which was played in his hometown of San Diego, the

Score! Football officials signal a touchdown by raising both arms straight up in the air.

Broncos put Terrell in the spotlight. On Denver's first drive, Davis carried the ball five times for 38 yards and scored on a 1-yard touchdown run.

Terrell scored twice in the AFC Championship Game.

Fumble
This occurs when a player drops the ball on the field. Either team can then recover it.

The Broncos scored on their next drive when Elway ran into the end zone on a 1-yard bootleg. Terrell ran for 27 yards on that drive, but was hit hard near the goal line.

"I blacked out for a minute," Terrell said. Denver's go-to guy suffered a severe headache and did not play in the second quarter.

Without him, Denver struggled to move the ball and only led the Packers 17-14 at halftime.

Helped by a trainer, Terrell left the game with a headache.

Terrell went to the locker room and took some medicine.

"Man, we really need you," Broncos tackle Tony Jones told Terrell during halftime. "I know you have a headache, but you can have a headache tomorrow. We've got a Super Bowl to win here."

The medicine worked, and Terrell returned to the game. The Broncos' coaches even called a play for Terrell to start the third quarter.

But Terrell fumbled on his first carry. Green Bay tied the game 17-17 with a field goal after that turnover.

If missing the second quarter was not bad enough, Terrell had now made a fumble that led to points for the Packers.

Big guys
Tony Jones (above) was one of Denver's offensive linemen in 1997. These players block defensive players and help running backs like Terrell find room to run.

Touchdown!
Terrell (30, above center) dived over from the 1-yard line on this play to score in Super Bowl XXXII. It was the first of his Super Bowl-record 3 rushing touchdowns. All were from 1 yard out.

"I turned the fumble into a form of motivation," Terrell said. "I told myself, 'Terrell, this is the chance you've always wanted. Make the most of it.'

"And I did. From then on, I just enjoyed the rest of the afternoon."

Terrell dominated the rest of the way. He helped Denver control the ball and the clock by running for 92 yards and two touchdowns.

Terrell scored the game-winning touchdown on a 1-yard run with one minute and 42 seconds remaining in the game.

On that six-play drive, he carried the ball 5 times for 50 yards.

When it came time to select the Super Bowl most valuable player, Terrell was an easy choice.

"In my book, he's the best running back in the league, bar none," said Elway, who won his first Super Bowl after losing three earlier Super Bowls.

Super Bowl silver
The winning team in the Super Bowl receives the Vince Lombardi Trophy, named for the Packers' coach who led his team to victories in Super Bowls I and II.

"I kept saying to our guys, 'He's looking to cut back, he's not running to the sideline,'" Green Bay Packers safety Eugene Robinson said after the game. "'So just hang back, hang back.' But Terrell got hit hard and just kept going."

Emmitt Smith set a record with 25 touchdowns in 1995.

Touchdown champions
Only two players have scored more touchdowns in a season than Terrell in 1998.

John Riggins scored 24 touchdowns in 1983.

Star still rising

The Denver Broncos and Terrell Davis entered the 1998 season determined to repeat as NFL champions.

With Terrell leading the way, the Broncos were almost unbeatable in 1998. Denver won its first 13 games of the season, but lost to the New York Giants in game 14 and the Miami Dolphins in game 15.

The Broncos finished the regular season with a 14-2 record and earned home-field advantage throughout the playoffs.

In 1998, Terrell led the league with 2,008 rushing yards, the third-highest single-season total in NFL history.

He also scored 23 touchdowns, the most ever by a Denver Broncos' player in one season, and the third most ever in NFL history.

"One of the biggest moments in my career came in our game against Seattle in 1998," Terrell said. "I was getting close to 2,000 yards, and the fans in Denver stood up and chanted 'T.D.! T.D.! T.D.!'"

Mile High Stadium literally shook as the fans rained down cheers on their hero, who had come a long way from San Diego.

Milestone
Only Terrell, Eric Dickerson, Barry Sanders, and O.J. Simpson have run for more than 2,000 yards in a season.

Terrell's running style combines speed and power.

Terrell had his best game of the regular season gainst the Seattle Seahawks in October, with 208 yards.

Taking the field
Before a game, NFL players are introduced to the fans, then run onto the field through a tunnel formed by teammates.

Terrell, who rushed for more than 100 yards in each of 11 games, was chosen as the NFL's most valuable player in 1998.

He helped his team defeat Miami 38-3 in the AFC divisional playoffs by rushing for 199 yards and 2 touchdowns in the first three quarters!

In Denver's 23-10 victory over the New York Jets in the AFC Championship Game, Terrell had 167 rushing yards and 1 touchdown.

Next up: Super Bowl XXXIII in Miami.

Denver won its second Super Bowl in a row by defeating the Atlanta Falcons 34-19.

"Super Bowl XXXII was a good win," Terrell said. "But I think Super Bowl XXXIII was better because we had to fight to win every game."

Terrell had made it. Many people thought he would not succeed, but he showed them all. What skills made him a great NFL player? Read on to find out.

Speedy
Only three other players reached 5,000 career rushing yards faster than Terrell.

Speed isn't everything

The scouting combine
In March, top college players gather to work out for NFL scouts, trying to impress them with speed and strength.

The 40
Coach Paul Brown started timing NFL players in the 40-yard dash in the 1950s; that was the distance a player would run to cover a punt.

After his senior year in college, Terrell Davis ran the 40-yard dash in 4.7 seconds for NFL scouts. He was one of the slowest running backs at the NFL Scouting Combine.

Most NFL teams like running backs to run 40 yards in 4.4 or 4.5 seconds. But a stopwatch could not measure Terrell's heart or his desire to play in the NFL.

"I don't think Terrell would finish in the top five on our team in the forty-yard dash," Broncos wide receiver Rod Smith said. "He's not the fastest guy around. But when he is running with the ball it is a different story. He would win the forty-yard dash carrying the ball."

"I'm a better player with pads on," Davis said. "I'm faster with pads on. You can't simulate game action by getting in starting blocks and having somebody yell 'go.'"

Terrell spends a lot of time talking to reporters about how he and the Broncos are doing.

"In a race, I cannot get the same intensity that I have on the field. I do not care what kind of speed I have. I'm fast enough when I want to be."

Some of Terrell's special skills that make up for his lack of speed include excellent quickness, great vision, good concentration, and a lot of poise.

Off the field, his outgoing personality has helped him win many fans, as well as work in advertisements.

On your mark... Track runners use these starting blocks to brace their feet before sprint races.

Helpers
Medical experts called "trainers" (white shirts, below) work with NFL players to help them stay safe and recover from injuries.

"I think concentration and poise are my greatest strengths," Terrell said. "Poise is a big thing in a game. If you get frustrated early in a game because you're not getting a lot of yards, you have to be poised and patient in order to keep working hard.

"I never blow a fuse during the game. I'm always thinking that things are going to get better."

Terrell's greatest quality might be his toughness. And probably the toughest things he has had to battle are migraine [MY-grane] headaches.

Terrell has suffered from these severe headaches since he was seven.

Migraines make his head throb and his body ache.

The first sign of a migraine comes when Terrell has trouble seeing and his vision becomes blurry. He knows that in 30 to 45 minutes a migraine

headache is coming. Sometimes they come in the middle of a game.

The migraines are usually caused by exertion. Whenever he lifts weights or plays sports, there is a chance he will get a migraine. But there also have been times when Terrell has gotten a migraine while he is just sitting down.

Breathe easy NFL players can receive oxygen on the sidelines (above), which helps them recover faster from their hard work on the field.

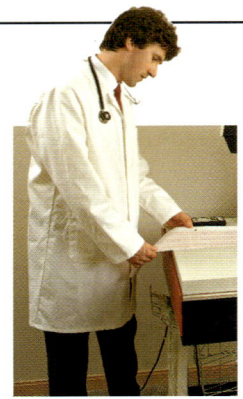

Specialist
Terrell went to specialists called neurologists, who use medicines to help patients with diseases of the brain and nervous system.

Tough tackle
Defensive players (41, left) stop play by knocking the ball carrier to the ground. This is called a "tackle."

"When I got migraines as a kid, I would have to run home, go into my room, turn off all the lights, and make sure the room was cool," Terrell said. "I couldn't control when I got them.

"When I first got a migraine I thought I was going blind. The pain was so bad, I kept thinking to myself, 'If this is what I have to go through, then I don't want to live.'"

Terrell deals with the problem in many ways.

He has seen neurologists [new-ROL-uh-jists], taken medication, had his wisdom teeth pulled, and worn braces to correct his bite.

Since joining the Broncos, Terrell has used a special nasal spray that helps stop migraine pain.

He also takes another pill given by doctors before games to prevent the headaches from starting.

"I pride myself on being tough," Terrell said. "I always wanted to be a lineman because they get to hit somebody on every play.

"I love the contact. Unless something is broken, and I can't walk, there's no way I'm going to come out of the game."

Tape it up Before practice and games, Terrell and other NFL players wrap their ankles in tape for stability.

Most valuable person

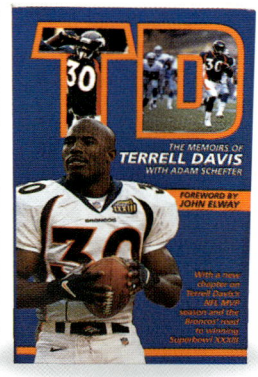

Terrell Davis has become a celebrity on and off the field.

He has appeared on many television shows, including one of his favorites, *Sesame Street.*

Terrell, who wears the number 30, helped *Sesame Street* celebrate its thirtieth anniversary. He sang a song with Big Bird, argued with Elmo, and counted numbers with the Count.

The star running back also had fun doing television commercials. Everywhere he goes, people ask him for his autograph.

But Terrell still remains a reserved person who doesn't like being in the spotlight. And he hasn't let success go to his head.

"Just because people perceive you as a superstar, you don't have to carry yourself in that manner," Terrell said.

"I'm not like that. You don't have to walk around like you're some kind of hotshot."

For example, after winning the MVP award in Super Bowl XXXII, he didn't go out to celebrate. He spent time with his family.

Terrell was given a Ford Mustang GT car for being named the MVP. Instead of putting the top down and driving in it, he gave the car to his brother Reggie.

Invalid
A person with a serious disease or disability who can't care for him- or herself and who needs help from others.

Terrell has been able to maintain balance in his life. He has his priorities in the right place.

When Terrell's great-grandfather Nishel suffered a stroke in 1984 and had to stay in bed, Terrell would feed Nishel and bathe him.

"Pops was an invalid," Terrell said. "He needed a lot of care. Taking care of him taught me responsibility at an early age."

In the past two years, Terrell has started the

Terrell Davis Salute the Kids Foundation, and the Terrell Davis Migraine Foundation. He has also spoken to the U.S. Congress about the need for more local parks.

In 1999, Terrell seriously injured his knee in the fourth game and was forced to miss the rest of the season.

"It was tough to sit and watch," Terrell said. "I've never had to go through an injury in my pro career.

"Not being able to play football has made me appreciate it. I have a new love for the game."

A big help Terrell's foundations help to find a cure for migraine headaches, and also help kids in need.

Terrell Davis has achieved great success in only six years. Many great players have NFL careers that last more than 10 years, so Terrell isn't ready to slow down.

In fact, he is ready to lead the Broncos to another Super Bowl championship!

Terrell and his mom met Sen. Frank Murkowski.

Congress quote "I remember how important parks were to me growing up," Terrell told the senators. "Kids today need parks even more."

Glossary

Accountant
A person who works with financial records, making sure they are accurate and up-to-date.

Cornerback
A defensive position responsible for covering opposing receivers.

End zone
Ten-yard areas at each end of a football field in which touchdowns are scored.

Fumble
Happens when a player carrying the football drops it on the field of play. Can be recovered by either team.

NFL Draft
Annual event at which NFL teams choose college players.

Nose guard
Defensive position in the middle of the defensive line, opposite the offensive team's center.

Pro Bowl
The NFL's all-star game, held each February in Hawaii.

Quarterback
The key offensive position; calls plays, makes passes and handoffs.

Rookie
A player in his first NFL season.

Running back
Offensive player who starts behind quarterback. Runs with ball, catches passes, and helps block defenders.

Scholarship
School fees that are paid by the school or by a charity.

Special teams
Units of NFL teams that participate in kickoff and punt coverage and on field-goal and extra-point attempts.

Super Bowl
The NFL's Championship Game, played each January between the AFC and NFC champions.

Touchdown
Six-point scoring play in which the football is caught in or carried into the end zone.

Transfer
When a student changes schools, sometimes to continue an athletic career.

Wild card
A team that doesn't finish in first place, but has a record good enough to make the NFL playoffs.

Index